Beating the Odds

A CHAPTER BOOK

BY MARY PACKARD

children's press ®

A Division of Scholastic Inc.
New York   Toronto   London   Auckland   Sydney
Mexico City   New Delhi   Hong Kong
Danbury, Connecticut

For Justin and Kate

ACKNOWLEDGMENTS

The author would like to thank everyone who gave their time and knowledge
to help with the research for this book. In particular, special thanks to
Karly Duncan, Marla Runyan, and Tom Whittaker.

Library of Congress Cataloging-in-Publication Data

Packard, Mary.
  Beating the odds : a chapter book / by Mary Packard.
    p. cm. – (True tales)
  Includes bibliographical references and index.
  ISBN 0-516-23731-4 (Lib. Bdg.)   0-516-24682-8 (Pbk.)
  1. Athletes with disabilities–United States–Biography–Juvenile literature.
  2. Athletes–United States–Biography–Juvenile literature. I. Title. II. Series.

GV697.A1P2814 2004
796'.087'092273–dc22

                        2004000417

1 2 3 4 5 6 7 8 9 10 R 13 12 11 10 09 08 07 06 05 04

CONTENTS

INTRODUCTION

You are about to meet four extraordinary athletes. They have all faced challenges that few of us can imagine. Each of them has overcome a physical **disability**.

As a child, Wilma Rudolph walked with a leg brace. Years later, she won three Olympic gold medals in running. Lance Armstrong, one of the world's best **cyclists**, battled **cancer** and came back stronger than ever. Marla Runyan is among the fastest women runners today despite being **legally blind**. Tom Whittaker lost his foot in an accident but that didn't stop him from climbing to the top of the world's highest mountain.

All these people have worked hard to reach their goals. All became the very best athletes they could be. They have set records that many non-disabled people can only dream of reaching.

CHAPTER ONE

THE TENNESSEE TORNADO

"Wilma! Wilma!" The crowds of people in Rome's Olympic Stadium shouted the name of their favorite African American runner. It was September 7, 1960. Two days before, Wilma Rudolph had won her second Olympic gold medal. Now she was trying for a third. That day, it was over 100 degrees Fahrenheit (38 degrees Celsius) in Rome, Italy. The heat didn't stop thousands of fans from coming out to root for Wilma.

Wilma Rudolph

Wilma became known as the Tennessee Tornado.

Wilma was running in the 400-meter relay. In this kind of race, four team members take turns running. When one runner is finished, she passes a stick called a **baton** (buh-TON) to the next runner in line. When it was Wilma's turn to take the baton, she almost dropped it. She lost speed. Worse still, after the two earlier races, Wilma's ankle was sore and swollen.

Wilma had made up her mind to win. She pushed herself to run faster. One by one, she passed the other runners. The crowd roared as Wilma crossed the finish line. Wilma Rudolph had won three gold medals in the same Olympics. No American woman runner had ever done that before. What made her **accomplishment** even more remarkable was that ten years before she could barely walk.

Wilma poses with her three gold medals.

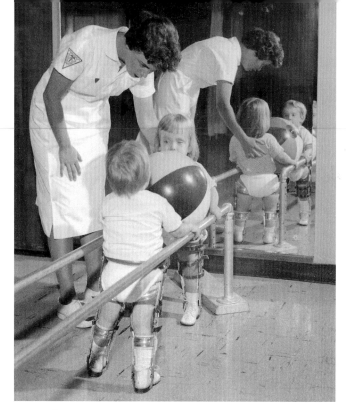

**Physical therapy helped children
with polio get better.**

Wilma Rudolph was born in Tennessee on
June 23, 1940. Her father was a railroad porter,
and her mother was a maid. Wilma was the
twentieth child in her family. They lived in a
small cottage in a town called Clarksville.

Wilma was born two months early.
Weighing only 4 pounds (2 kilograms), she
was tiny and weak. As a baby and a young
child, Wilma got one illness after another.
Blanche, Wilma's mother, always nursed her
daughter back to health.

When she was four, Wilma got very sick. She had a high fever. Her left leg became so weak and twisted that she couldn't use it. Doctors told Wilma's parents that their daughter had a disease called **polio** (POH-lee-oh). Wilma might never walk again. Her only hope was to get **physical therapy** (FIZ-uh-kuhl THER-uh-PEE).

The nearest hospital was in Nashville, 50 miles (80 kilometers) away. That didn't stop Blanche from taking her daughter there. They traveled by bus twice a week. The doctors pushed and pulled Wilma's crooked leg. They moved it round and round in circles over and over again. The therapy hurt. Wilma tried not to cry. She tried to think of happy things. One day she hoped to play sports with her brothers and sisters.

After two years, Wilma's leg started to get better. Now Blanche could treat Wilma at home. Wilma's brothers and sisters took turns helping their mother with Wilma's therapy.

By the time she was seven, Wilma could walk with a leg brace. Wilma hated her

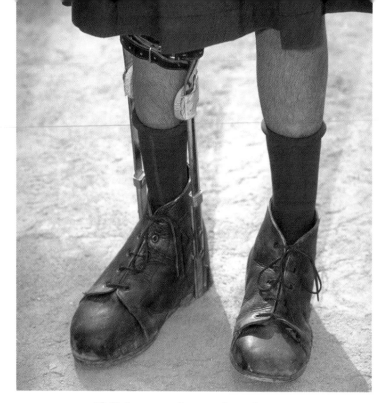

Child wearing a leg brace

heavy brace. She made up her mind to fight her illness. She would practice walking without her brace no matter how much it hurt.

Wilma's hard work paid off. When she was ten, she could walk a short distance without her brace. Two years later, she could walk and run on her own.

At last Wilma was ready to play sports. In high school, she became the star player on the girl's basketball team. C. C. Gray, her coach, called her "Skeeter," short for mosquito. He said it was because she was little, fast, and always in the way.

One day a famous college track coach saw Wilma play. His name was Ed Temple. Coach Temple invited Wilma to train with his track team that summer. Soon Wilma was traveling to races all around the country. At sixteen, she made the Olympic track team. Although she was the team's youngest member, Wilma earned a bronze medal as a runner in a relay.

After high school, Coach Temple helped Wilma get a full **scholarship** (SKOL-ur-ship) to college. That meant that she could go to college for free. Wilma worked hard at her studies and at her running, too. In 1960, she made the Olympic team again. This time she won three gold medals. She was now the fastest woman in the world.

To celebrate her victory, Buford Ellington, the governor of Tennessee, planned a parade. At that time Tennessee was **segregated** (SEG-ruh-gated). The governor ruled that only white people were allowed to see the parade. Wilma said she would not come unless everyone was invited. The parade was held the way Wilma wanted it.

In 1962, Wilma retired from racing. She became a teacher and a high school coach. She also started the Wilma Rudolph Foundation to raise money for children in poor neighborhoods. Because of her work, many promising athletes have been given a chance at beating the odds.

In 1994, at age fifty-four, Wilma Rudolph died. Her life continues to inspire young people all over the world.

Wilma coaches her daughter, Yolanda.

CHAPTER TWO

RIDING TO VICTORY

Each year the biggest names in bicycle racing come to Austin, Texas. They come to compete in Ride for the Roses, a contest that helps raise money for finding a cure for cancer. All the racers want to win, of course. In 1998, Lance Armstrong, one of the world's best cyclists, had a special reason. It was his first race since he had been cured of cancer. For most of the race, Lance stayed with the other cyclists. He wanted to save his energy for the end.

Lance Armstrong

Lance sprinting to the finish line

With just one lap to go, Lance pedaled ahead of the group. He picked up speed, leaving the other cyclists behind. One last sprint and he was over the finish line. He had beaten all 5,000 cyclists!

More than a year before the race, Lance Armstrong was riding in the 138-mile (222-kilometer) road race in the 1996 Olympics. Suddenly, he felt weak. His body ached. Even his eyesight was blurry.

After the race, Lance saw a doctor. The doctor ran some tests and told Lance that he had cancer. Lance could not believe what he had just heard. He was young. He was strong. He was fit. There must be some mistake.

There wasn't a mistake. The cancer had already spread to his lungs, to his stomach, and to his brain. Doctors told Lance that he had only one year to live.

Lance had other ideas. He would fight for his life with everything he had. After he had learned all he could about his disease, he made some decisions.

First, he had operations to cut out the cancer. Next, he started **chemotherapy** (kee-moh-THER-uh-pee) treatments. Chemotherapy is very strong medicine. It is strong enough to kill cancer cells. While it is doing its job, it can make a person very sick. Lance's hair fell out and he lost 20 pounds (9 kilograms). When Lance went on bike rides between his treatments, sometimes he would run out of breath. A few times he had to call for help.

Lance hopes that cancer will one day be cured.

During his chemotherapy treatments,
Lance met many other people with cancer.
He wanted to do something to help them. He
started the Lance Armstrong Foundation to
help find a cure for cancer.

After his chemotherapy, Lance got stronger each day. In the spring of 1997, doctors took new tests. Chest X-rays and a blood test showed that Lance was cancer free.

Once Lance was cured of cancer, he concentrated on getting back in shape. He had lost a lot of weight. He decided he would build up his body in a new way. He worked to make the muscles in his legs and shoulders strong. Strong but thin, he now had the perfect body for cycling.

After winning the Ride for the Roses, Lance began to train for the Tour de France. In Europe, bicycle riding is as popular as football is in America. For people who live there, the Tour de France is like the Super Bowl.

The race takes three weeks and covers more than 2,000 miles (3,219 kilometers). The cyclists ride up steep mountains and race down at speeds of 70 miles (113 kilometers) per hour. The conditions are often dangerous.

Lance's training had gotten him in great shape. He was ready to race in the Tour de France. Not only that, he intended to win.

At the beginning of the race, everyone wondered if Lance could do it. By the end, they wondered if there was anything he couldn't do. On the twentieth day of the race, more than 500,000 people were waiting for Lance. They shouted his name as he sped past them. They cheered as he crossed the finish line. The cyclist everyone thought would win the race, Alex Zulle of Switzerland, came in more than seven minutes after Lance.

Since then, Lance Armstrong has continued to win. So far he has won five Tour de France races in a row. He hopes that his comeback will inspire other people who have cancer not to give up.

Lance holds up his prize.

CHAPTER THREE

KEEPING UP WITH MARLA

The women's 1,500-meter race at the Olympic trials in Sacramento, California, was about to begin. Marla Runyan took her place at the starting line. At the trials, athletes compete against the best athletes from their own country to see who will make the Olympic team. More than anything, Marla wanted to be a member of the United States Olympic track team.

Marla Runyan

2000 U.S. OLYMPIC TEAM TRIALS
TRACK AND FIELD

796

SACRAMENTO

2000 U.S. OLYMPIC TE
TRACK AND FI

21

SACR

25

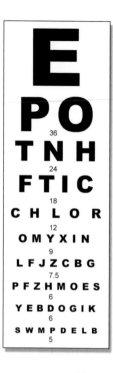

Like the other runners on the starting line, Marla had run countless miles. She had run when she was hurt and when no one thought she could win. Unlike the other runners, though, Marla was legally blind in both eyes. Although Marla has some sight, she isn't able to see the big letter *E* on the eye chart.

Minutes before the race started, Marla had been putting ice on her injured leg. She had pulled a **ligament** (LIG-uh-muhnt) in that leg several months earlier while she was running. Although her leg still hurt, she tried not to think about it.

"The future has not been written," she whispered, "and I am in control." As always, those words made her feel calm.

The first two laps were a blur. On the third lap, the runner in front of Marla stumbled. Somehow Marla managed not to run into her.

Marla was in sixth place. A bell rang for the last lap. Marla picked up her speed.

Within seconds, she was over the finish line. Marla Runyan had just become the first legally blind athlete to make it to the Olympics.

Marla is leading the race.

Marla as a young girl

When Marla was nine, her world began to get dark. In school she had trouble seeing the blackboard. At home, she had trouble reading, even when she held the book up to her nose. Marla spent a lot of time in doctors' offices. They could find nothing wrong. One doctor even thought Marla could really see and was only pretending to have eye problems.

At last a doctor came up with a **diagnosis** (dye-uhg-NOH-siss). Marla had **Stargardt's Disease**, a rare disease that attacks a person's **retina** (RET-uhn-uh). Doctors told Marla's parents that Marla would never be able to keep up with the other children in school. She would probably not be able to go to college, nor would she ever play sports.

The doctors didn't know how hard Marla could work. Marla refused to give in to her blindness. Her parents saw to it that she didn't have to. They got her a monocular, a special telescope to help her see the blackboard. They also got her a giant reading machine that could make letters look bigger on a television screen.

Marla's brother Grady helped, too. When it was time for Marla to go to high school, he took Marla all

Monocular

around the building so she could memorize the position of her classrooms.

Marla training

Marla got so good at getting around that it was hard to tell that she was blind. Some people thought that she was snobbish when she didn't say hello. They didn't know that Marla couldn't see them.

The track was one place where Marla did not have to worry about bumping into things. When she was running, she felt free. She didn't need a monocular to do well. In fact, she did so well in track and in the classroom that she got a scholarship to college. She graduated in 1991. In 1994, she got her master's degree so that she could teach deaf and blind children.

Outside of the classroom, Marla worked to become an Olympic athlete. She moved to Eugene, Oregon, to get the best training. Eugene is often called "Track City" because so many runners and trainers live there.

Then, just five weeks before the Olympic trials, Marla pulled the ligament in her left leg. Instead of giving up, she had physical therapy. Then she trained even harder.

Her work paid off. Marla became one of the members of the United States track team chosen to compete in the 2000 Summer Olympics in Sydney, Australia. Although she didn't win a medal there, Marla was the eighth fastest female runner in the 1,500-meter race.

Marla plans to compete again in the 2004 Olympic games. When doctors discovered that Marla was legally blind, they thought that she would have trouble keeping up with other children. They were so wrong. Now everyone else is trying to keep up with Marla!

Marla crosses the finish line.

CHAPTER FOUR

CLIMBING TO THE TOP

In 1979, Tom Whittaker, a **mountaineer**, lost his right foot in a car accident. An out-of-control car had swerved out of its lane and hit Tom's car head on. Tom was badly hurt. Both of his legs were shattered. His right foot had to be **amputated** and he lost one of his kneecaps.

Tom's doctors told him that he would never be able to walk. Tom did not accept their diagnosis. Not only did he plan to walk again, he planned to climb Mount Everest.

Thousands of people have tried to make it to the top of the world's tallest mountain. Most have failed.

Tom Whittaker

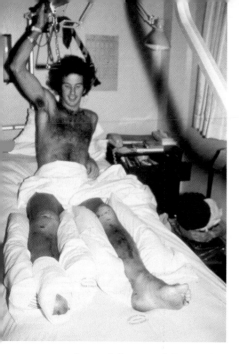

Tom after his accident

Tom fought hard to recover. As soon as he learned how to walk on his artificial foot, he taught himself to climb again.

In the spring of 1989, ten years after his accident, Tom made his first attempt at Mount Everest. He came to the **Himalayas** (him-uh-LAY-uhz) with a friend and two guides called **Sherpas** (SHER-puhz).

The men began their climb up the mountain. The mountain is 29,035 feet (8,850 meters) tall. After weeks of climbing, Tom's group had made it to 24,000 feet (7,315 meters).

Suddenly, without warning, the sky turned dark. A storm was coming. Tom and the other men struggled to put up their tent. Icy snow stung their faces, and wind blew them to their knees. They huddled in their

Yaks help carry supplies up the mountain.

tent until the storm was over. The snow came up to their waists.

The men cut snowshoes for themselves out of the plastic packaging that held their supplies. The cold made the plastic brittle, and the shoes snapped in two.

The group could not go on. They left their gear and supplies on the mountain and made their way back to the base. They were lucky to escape with their lives. Seven climbers had already died on the mountain that year.

Although he didn't make it to the top on his first try, six years later Tom came back to try again. This time Tom got even closer to the top. Then another storm hit, and once again, Tom had to turn back.

Mountain climbing presents many dangers even to people who are not disabled. **Avalanches** (AV-uh-lan-chez), blizzards, and freezing cold temperatures have caused hundreds of injuries and deaths.

The higher a climber goes, the less oxygen there is to breathe. Without enough oxygen, climbers can get dizzy and weak, so many climbers carry oxygen tanks.

A person with one foot uses twice as much energy and oxygen as a climber who has two feet. That didn't stop Tom from making his third attempt at the mountain.

Tom wears spikes on his boots to
keep from slipping on the ice.

To prepare for his climbs, Tom trained on treadmills and lifted weights. He made sure he had plenty of rest, ate healthful meals, and took vitamins.

On his third try, Tom made it over patches of ice. He pulled himself up steep cliffs and crossed slippery mountain passes. Below him were deep, jagged drops. On May 27, 1998, Tom looked up and saw

Tom's family traveled part of the way with him.

Tom on skis

there was no mountain left to climb. One
more step and a final pull, and Tom had
made history. He was the first **amputee**
(AM-pyuh-tee) to climb to the top of
Mount Everest.

After he returned from Mount Everest,
Tom decided to help other disabled people

Tom helps a man in a wheelchair get safely down a mountain.

reach their goals. He started the Windhorse Legacy, a foundation that raises money to support programs for the disabled. Tom Whittaker believes, "It's not the falling down, but the getting up that matters."

GLOSSARY

accomplishment something that is done successfully

amputate to cut off or remove

amputee (AM-pyuh-tee) someone disabled because a body part has been removed

avalanche (AV-uh-lanch) a large amount of snow, ice, earth, or rocks that suddenly falls down a mountain

baton (buh-TON) a stick that is carried and then passed on by each runner of a relay race

cancer a disease in which cells multiply out of control

chemotherapy (kee-moh-THER-uh-pee) a treatment that uses drugs to fight cancer

cyclist a bicycle rider

diagnosis (dye-uhg-NOH-siss) the act of figuring out why someone is sick

disability (diss-uh-BIL-uh-tee) a problem with your body or mind that stops you from doing what you want to do

Himalayas (him-uh-LAY-uhz) a mountain range in South Asia

legally blind not able to see well enough to read an eye chart

ligament (LIG-uh-muhnt) a band of strong tissue that connects bones

mountaineer a person who climbs mountains

physical therapy (FIZ-uh-kuhl THER-uh-PEE) a treatment that features exercise

polio (POH-lee-oh) a disease that attacks the brain and spinal cord

retina (RET-uhn-uh) an inner layer of the eye that is sensitive to light

scholarship (SKOL-ur-ship) money given to a person to pay for college

segregated (SEG-ruh-gated) divided or separated by race

Sherpa (SHER-puh) a person from Tibet who lives in the Himalayas

Stargardt's Disease an eye disease that damages the retina

FIND OUT MORE

The Tennessee Tornado
http://espn.go.com/sportscentury/features/00016446.html
Read a newspaper article from 1960 that tells how Wilma
Rudolph won her three gold medals.

Riding to Victory
www.lancearmstrong.com
See photos of Lance Armstrong racing and read his
biography.

Keeping Up With Marla
www.marlarunyan.com
Take a peek at Marla Runyan's journal. You can also learn
more about Stargardt's Disease at this website.

Climbing to the Top
www.tomwhittaker.com
Tom Whittaker's website has more information about his
climb up Mount Everest.

More Books to Read

Lance Armstrong: The Race of His Life by Kristin Armstrong,
Penguin Putnam Books, 2000

No Finish Line: My Life As I See It by Marla Runyan,
G. P. Putnam's Sons, 2001

The Top of the World: Climbing Mount Everest
by Steve Jenkins, Houghton Mifflin, 2002

*Wilma Unlimited: How Wilma Rudolph Became the World's
Fastest Woman* by Kathleen Krull, 2000

INDEX

PHOTO CREDITS

MEET THE AUTHOR

 The author of more than 200 picture books, Mary Packard has been writing for children for as long as she can remember. She lives in Northport, New York, with her husband and her cat, Fraggle.

Packard read her first biography when she was in third grade. It was about a deaf and blind girl named Helen Keller. She enjoyed the book so much that she didn't stop until she had read every biography in the children's section of the library.

Packard believes that reading about how other people face challenges in their lives can inspire us to find new ways to cope with our own problems. It's also a fun way to try out things you might not think of doing in real life, like climbing a mountain, for instance.